THE
HAPPINESS
WORKBOOK
FOR KIDS

24 Fun Activities to Help
Kids Focus, Make Smart Choices,
and Bounce Back from Challenges

Maureen Healy

Copyright © 2022 by Maureen Healy

Published by
PESI Publishing, Inc.
3839 White Ave
Eau Claire, WI 54703

Cover: Amy Rubenzer
Editing: Jenessa Jackson, PhD
Layout: Baker & Taylor and Amy Rubenzer

ISBN: 9781683734949 (print)
ISBN: 9781683734956 (ePUB)
ISBN: 9781683734963 (ePDF)

All rights reserved.
Printed in the United States of America.

PESI Publishing
pesipublishing.com

Table of Contents

· · · · · · · · · · · · ·

SECTION 3: BECOMING HAPPIER

A Note to Adults

Do you want to feel happier? Do you wish your children were happier too? Can you imagine a school where the "how" of happier life experiences is part of the curriculum? Do you think children would benefit from emotional health and happiness instruction?

If you answered yes to any of these questions, *The Happiness Workbook for Kids* is for you. Inside this workbook is a new way for adults to teach children how to constructively express their emotions, develop resilience, and move toward happier life experiences. Intended for elementary and middle school–aged children, this workbook simplifies complex ideas so children can develop:

- Self-awareness
- Emotion regulation (for example, how to make smart choices!)
- Resilience
- Habits of happiness

Oftentimes, children have been taught the importance of external outcomes (e.g., grades, trophies, athleticism) versus inner outcomes (e.g., resilience, character, happier life experiences). Of course, academics and other activities are important, but they must be coupled with clear instruction on resilience and positive emotional health. That's because the happiest lives are built on the ability to bounce back from challenges and to use problems as stepping-stones toward a better life.

The Happiness Workbook for Kids gives you exactly what you need: a comprehensive toolkit to help children understand and make better choices with their emotions— even the tricky ones! As we know, children often feel things deeply and react quickly. Some of those reactions aren't always easy or helpful, such as when they slam doors or say mean things. By learning how emotions work and using the tools in this workbook, children can better understand their emotions and express them constructively (versus destructively).

This workbook is broken into three sections: Section 1 helps children understand the different types of emotions and how they work; section 2 helps them express their emotions constructively and make smart choices with them, no matter what; and section 3 focuses on helping children become happier. Most parents, teachers, and other caring adults simply want to see their children become happier. But let's be clear: This isn't about some pie-in-the-sky happiness. It's about helping children cultivate real-life skills they can use to become happier by overcoming the challenges and moving toward better experiences.

This book is written in language that children in early grade school can understand, so they should be able to complete most of the activities on their own. However, they may have questions and need some assistance. My suggestion is to make yourself available while they are completing the activities and to have a meaningful dialogue about the topic afterward.

Using this workbook will help your children and students make better choices with their emotions and move toward happier life experiences. Becoming more resilient and developing skills of positive emotional health will take time and practice, but rest assured—you're helping these children feel, and ultimately do, their best.

Best wishes,
Maureen Healy

Introduction for Kids

Someone gave you this book because you feel big emotions. They want you to be happier and have an easier time managing your feelings. No one is born knowing how to handle their emotions—they learn through experience, teachers, or books like this.

In this book, you'll learn how to:

- Create positive emotions
- Bounce back from challenges
- Make smart choices
- Move toward happier life experiences

Although dealing with your feelings isn't always easy, with continued practice, you can succeed. The truth is, children make the world a brighter place, and that certainly includes you!

1

Understanding Emotions

· · · · · · · · · · · · ·

In this section, you'll learn more about your emotions and about different types of emotions, including challenging emotions (like anger) and positive emotions (like happiness). The more you learn about different emotions, the easier it becomes to make smart choices when you feel each of them.

Activity 1

What Are Emotions?

HAPPINESS LESSON

Emotions point to how you're feeling inside, like happy, mad, grateful, or grumpy. Learning how to notice your emotions is the first step to becoming happier.

There are many different emotions, which you can feel at any time.

Like Emma: *She shared her lunch with a new classmate, Lizzie, who forgot her lunch money. The act of sharing made Emma feel happier.*

Emotions show you how you feel inside. They are not good or bad, but they can indicate what direction you're heading.

Like Anna: *She cheated on her spelling test. Anna knew it was wrong, and she felt terrible afterward.*

Emotions that make you feel upset often indicate it's time to do something differently, and for Anna that was true.

Like Joey: *He missed his class field trip because of an important hospital visit. Joey felt disappointed that he missed out.*

Of course, some emotions aren't as simple as feeling happy or sad. They are complex. Joey was bummed to miss the field trip, but he was also happy that his visit to the hospital was a success. He feels good and realizes that his health is the most important thing right now.

Understanding how to identify your emotions—and how to make smart choices with them—is our work together in this book.

Copyright © 2022 Maureen Healy. *The Happiness Workbook for Kids.* All rights reserved.

To Do

There are many different emotions. Some moments you may feel happy and silly, while other times you might feel frustrated and angry. Column A lists different emotions you might have had. Column B lists synonyms (words that mean the same thing) for those emotions. Draw a line from each feeling in Column A to its synonyms in Column B.

Column A	Column B
Sad	Enthusiastic, eager
Angry	Courageous, strong
Happy	Timid, bashful
Frustrated	Joyful, glad
Brave	Awkward, humiliated
Excited	Unhappy, blue
Scared	Sure of oneself, cool
Shy	Interested, eager to learn
Sleepy	Tired, fatigued
Embarrassed	Giving, sharing
Confident	Mad, furious
Curious	Afraid, fearful
Generous	Irritated, annoyed

(When you see this image, it means you can find the answers to this activity in the answer key in the back of the book.)

Copyright © 2022 Maureen Healy. *The Happiness Workbook for Kids.* All rights reserved.

... And More to Do

Look at the following pictures. For each one, write what the person is doing and what emotions they are showing.

_____

_____

_____

_____

_____

_____

_____

_____

Copyright © 2022 Maureen Healy. _The Happiness Workbook for Kids._ All rights reserved.

Ideas to Remember

Emotions are signs of how you're feeling inside. There are no bad emotions either—they're simply sending a message to say, "Hi, I am happy" or "Hi, I am angry." Being able to name each emotion helps you recognize what is really happening so you can make a smart choice about what to do with that emotion.

Of course, you can have mixed emotions too. There may be moments when you feel angry and sad, or happy and nervous, at the same time. That's normal. Most people feel more than one emotion at times too.

Copyright © 2022 Maureen Healy. *The Happiness Workbook for Kids*. All rights reserved.

Activity 2

What Are Thoughts?

. . . .

HAPPINESS LESSON

Thoughts are the ideas and opinions you have about yourself and the world around you. They happen in your mind. You can learn to pick your thoughts on purpose.

. . . .

Thoughts are the things you think in your mind. You may have hundreds or even thousands of thoughts a day. Your thoughts can change quickly too. One morning you may wake up and think, "This is a great day," but when you go outside, a car drives by and splashes mud all over you. Now you might think, "This day stinks." Or maybe you laugh and think, "This is the funniest thing ever."

You are the only one who can think your thoughts. Some thoughts (like feelings) feel better than others. If you were to think, "This is the funniest thing ever," it probably would feel better than if you thought, "This day stinks" when mud was covering you from head to toe.

It is also helpful to understand that thoughts and emotions are different. Your thoughts are ideas that pass through your mind. They are always changing. Your emotions are feelings that you experience, like scared, happy, or silly. They are always changing too.

You can learn to pick your thoughts on purpose and focus your thinking in whatever direction you choose.

Copyright © 2022 Maureen Healy. *The Happiness Workbook for Kids.* All rights reserved.

To Do

Children like yourself have many different thoughts throughout the day. And different situations in life may cause you to think different thoughts. Read through each of the examples below, and then imagine what you would think if you were in that situation. (Remember to focus on thoughts, not feelings.)

Gaby drops her books down the stairs at school. Her classmates all laugh.

What would you think if you were Gaby?

_____

_____

Bella's coach announced to the team that they made it to the playoffs. She's worked so hard for this.

What would you think if you were Bella?

_____

_____

José was playing in a soccer match when his pants split. His teammates all made funny faces, and his coach sent him off the field to change his pants.

What would you think if you were José?

_____

_____

Sean tried out for the school play and got one of the lead roles. He practiced so much to get this role!

What would you think if you were Sean?

_____

_____

Copyright © 2022 Maureen Healy. *The Happiness Workbook for Kids.* All rights reserved.

... And More to Do

Thoughts, like feelings, are not good or bad. They just *are*. Learning to stop and then choose thoughts that make you feel better takes practice. For example, Gaby, who dropped her books in front of her class, might have thought, "This is the worst thing ever," which would feel terrible. Or she might have thought, "Everybody drops things sometimes," which would feel better.

Here are more of Gaby's thoughts from that day. Circle the thoughts that are more positive.

I'm awesome.

School stinks.

I hate chores, especially cleaning my room.

I'm talented at playing the piano.

I'm getting better at math.

My parents are embarrassing.

The school uniforms are scratchy and itchy.

I forgot to feed my goldfish.

I can't wait to play video games.

These shoes are the worst.

The lights are too bright.

I love music class.

My art project might win the contest.

My brother is annoying.

Copyright © 2022 Maureen Healy. *The Happiness Workbook for Kids*. All rights reserved.

Ideas to Remember

Thoughts are the things you think inside your mind. They are often about yourself or other people in your life. You can learn to choose your thoughts on purpose with practice. If you've ever played a video game, practiced the piano, or learned how to kick a soccer ball into the net, you've probably given yourself a pep talk and said, "I can do this." That's choosing a positive thought on purpose.

Copyright © 2022 Maureen Healy. *The Happiness Workbook for Kids*. All rights reserved.

Activity 3

New Thought, New Feeling

HAPPINESS LESSON

Thoughts and feelings are connected. When you have a new thought, you get a new feeling. For example, if you think, "I've got no friends," you'll feel down in the dumps. But if you think, "I can make a new friend today," you'll feel a bit more positive.

Imagine that you're learning how to hula hoop and you keep dropping the hula hoop. You think, "I stink at hula hooping," which feels negative. But now imagine that your best friend comes along and smiles at you. Your friend says, "You can do it!" and gives you some tips. Soon you're thinking, "Wow, I'm really improving," and you feel more positive.

It is helpful to understand that when you think a new thought, you get a new feeling.

Of course, thoughts and feelings aren't always that simple. They can be complex. Like Taylor, who wanted to become a famous singer. She was sure of her singing ability, but she was afraid of performing on stage. Taylor thought, "I don't think I can do this!" Her thoughts were full of fear about singing in front of thousands of people.

Eventually, Taylor learned to think new thoughts, such as "I can do this," "I've got this," and "I was born to sing." This led to her feeling better about performing in front of others and being able to do it.

Copyright © 2022 Maureen Healy. *The Happiness Workbook for Kids.* All rights reserved.

To Do

Every thought produces a feeling. Sometimes you naturally think positive thoughts that make you feel happy, excited, generous, and grateful. Other times you think more negative thoughts for a variety of reasons, and they don't feel as good. You can learn to choose your thoughts so you can grow stronger and happier.

Read the examples below, and circle the thoughts that would help these kids feel better.

Sophia is practicing for soccer tryouts. She keeps thinking, "I'm no good," which makes her feel bad. Circle the thoughts that can help her feel better.

I'm terrible at soccer.

Everyone is bad in the beginning.

If I practice more, I'll get better.

Noah is new to his school, and he is very shy. He keeps thinking, "I don't know anyone" and "I'm all alone." Circle the thoughts that can help him feel better.

I'm brave today.

Nobody is going to be my friend.

I only need one friend to start.

Jemima doesn't understand why kids are picking on her for her accent. She speaks differently because her family is originally from England. Circle the thoughts that can help her feel better.

Kids can be mean.

They all sound funny to me too.

I'm going to make a friend who loves my accent.

Copyright © 2022 Maureen Healy. *The Happiness Workbook for Kids.* All rights reserved.

... And More to Do

Learning how to think a new thought when you're feeling negative takes practice—and perhaps some help in the beginning. Consider Charlotte: She got upset when her sister kept taking her special drawing tablet. Immediately, she would get angry, run into her sister's room, and say, "Give me my tablet back!"

But with help from her mom, Charlotte began thinking that her sister just wanted some more love, and maybe—just maybe—letting her sister borrow her drawing tablet wasn't a bad thing. Charlotte slowly changed her thinking, and she learned how to share her belongings with her little sister who looked up to her. This helped her feel more positive too.

Can you remember a time when you changed how you thought about something and began feeling better? If so, please share.

_____

_____

_____

_____

_____

_____

_____

_____

_____

_____

Copyright © 2022 Maureen Healy. *The Happiness Workbook for Kids.* All rights reserved.

Ideas to Remember

Thoughts and feelings are connected. Certain thoughts move you toward better feelings, and other thoughts move you in a more challenging and negative direction. The perfect example is when you're learning how to do something new, like ride a bike or scooter. On your first ride, you might fall off and think, "Oh no!" But after that first fall, you decide to think more positively and say, "I'm getting better with each try." Of course, this new thought feels much better too. That's why it's so important to learn how to choose your thoughts.

Copyright © 2022 Maureen Healy. *The Happiness Workbook for Kids.* All rights reserved.

Types of Emotions

HAPPINESS LESSON

Emotions can be positive (helpful) or negative (challenging). Our work is to learn how to increase the positive emotions and make smart choices when we have negative emotions.

Everyone has emotions. Your family members, friends, and teachers all have emotions ranging from sadness to joy. Of course, it feels better when you feel happy instead of sad! You naturally want to feel positive emotions, and that's normal. But there are also moments when you will feel angry or hurt. These are more challenging emotions that are a normal part of life.

When you "catch" your emotions (both the positive and negative ones) early on, it gives you a chance to slow down and then choose how to express them in a smart way.

Positive emotions feel good and benefit both you and others. Some examples are gratitude, generosity, love, and kindness. Negative emotions don't necessarily feel so good, and they can be challenging to express in a skillful and responsible way. Some examples are anger, sadness, jealousy, and disgust.

All emotions are useful. They send you signals that let you know how you feel inside. The goal isn't to simply increase positive emotions and get rid of negative emotions—the aim is to learn how to manage *all* your different feelings so you feel stronger and can skillfully handle any challenges while moving toward happier experiences.

Copyright © 2022 Maureen Healy. *The Happiness Workbook for Kids.* All rights reserved.

To Do

Lilly wants to get a dog more than anything. Her mom said if Lilly can keep her room clean for a month, she'll get a dog for her. Of course, this is a challenge for Lilly, but she feels positive she can do it. Circle the emotions you think Lilly feels now that getting a dog is possible.

Angry

Sad

Scared

Hopeful

Happy

Jealous

Focused

Excited

Silly

Thrilled

Enthusiastic

Are the emotions you circled positive or negative?

_____

Are there any more emotions that Lilly might feel about getting a dog?

_____

_____

_____

Copyright © 2022 Maureen Healy. *The Happiness Workbook for Kids*. All rights reserved.

... And More to Do

Children like you and Lilly feel positive as well as negative emotions. This is normal. You may even feel certain emotions more than others. Put a check mark by each of the different emotions listed here to show how often you feel that emotion.

	Often	Sometimes	Never
Angry	_____	_____	_____
Sad	_____	_____	_____
Happy	_____	_____	_____
Silly	_____	_____	_____
Scared	_____	_____	_____
Embarrassed	_____	_____	_____
Playful	_____	_____	_____
Tired	_____	_____	_____
Upset	_____	_____	_____
Thankful	_____	_____	_____
Afraid	_____	_____	_____
Excited	_____	_____	_____
Frustrated	_____	_____	_____
Misunderstood	_____	_____	_____
Loved	_____	_____	_____

Copyright © 2022 Maureen Healy. *The Happiness Workbook for Kids*. All rights reserved.

Ideas to Remember

Learning how to understand and handle all the different emotions is the work of our lives. In this activity, we discussed the two types of emotions:

- **Positive emotions:** These are *helpful* and bring benefit to yourself and others.

- **Negative emotions:** These are *challenging* emotions, which need to be skillfully handled to harm no one.

Of course, some emotions feel better than others, but again—there are no bad emotions. They are simply sending signs to how you're feeling inside. It's really what you do with them that matters.

Copyright © 2022 Maureen Healy. *The Happiness Workbook for Kids.* All rights reserved.

Activity 5

Emotions in the Body

HAPPINESS LESSON

Emotions are felt in your body. Every person gets unique "body signals" that show them how they're feeling inside, whether it's excitement, anger, or any other emotion. Learning how to spot our emotions in our bodies can help us make smart choices with them.

Our emotions are always changing. *Consider John*: One minute, he's happy because he's eating an ice cream cone in his favorite flavor. A few minutes later, a dog bumps into him, and he drops the ice cream cone on the street. He is now upset. Like John, we can go from happy to sad in a matter of seconds.

Take a look at the blank faces below. Read the emotion next to each face, and draw how that emotion feels on your face. Try to draw each one differently.

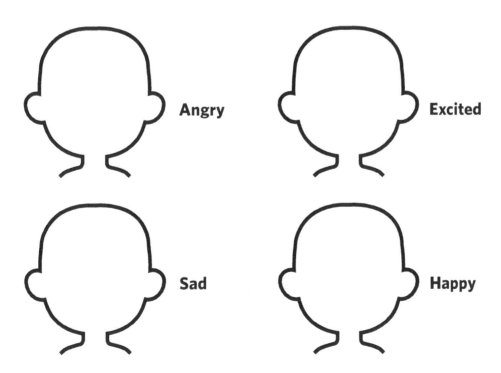

Copyright © 2022 Maureen Healy. *The Happiness Workbook for Kids.* All rights reserved.

To Do

Volcanoes are mountains with hot lava inside of them. Scientists study volcanoes and have found that they change before erupting. Some of the changes include getting hotter, swelling up, and having little earthquakes under them. Once the scientists spot these changes, they can tell people so they can leave the area and stay safe. Just like a volcano, you may feel physical changes in your body when you're feeling a negative emotion and want to erupt. For example, you may get warmer or clench your fists.

Some people listen well to their bodies. They learn to calm down before they erupt like a volcano. Most people are still learning, though. Look at the words listed here, and circle the place in your body where you feel each emotion.

Angry

Frustrated

Scared

Sad

Disgusted

Worried

Copyright © 2022 Maureen Healy. *The Happiness Workbook for Kids*. All rights reserved.

Scientists watch volcanoes all the time—not just when they are erupting, but also when they are calm. You can do the same thing with your body. You can start noticing when and where you feel positive emotions in your body too.

Once again, look at the words listed here, and circle the place in your body where you feel each emotion.

Calm

Excited

Thankful

Loved

Silly

Happy

Copyright © 2022 Maureen Healy. *The Happiness Workbook for Kids*. All rights reserved.

... And More to Do

Was it easy to remember where in your body you felt each emotion? Why or why not?

_____

_____

_____

_____

_____

Which emotions brought up good memories?

_____

_____

_____

_____

_____

Did any emotions bring up memories you didn't like? If so, which ones?

_____

_____

_____

_____

_____

Copyright © 2022 Maureen Healy. _The Happiness Workbook for Kids_. All rights reserved.

Ideas to Remember

We experience emotions in our bodies. Learning how to spot emotions in your body is helpful. For example, you may feel anger in your face, which gets red, and in your hands, which want to make fists. Or you may feel sadness in your tummy and get a tummy ache. Becoming aware of how you experience each emotion in your body helps you catch the emotion when it's small (like frustration) versus big (like anger). Of course, we may erupt like a volcano sometimes too—but if we can learn to handle it better, that's a good thing.

Copyright © 2022 Maureen Healy. *The Happiness Workbook for Kids*. All rights reserved.

Activity 6

Emotions in the World

HAPPINESS LESSON

We feel emotions on the inside but show them on the outside. Positive emotions in your body can turn into smiles, handshakes, hugs, and sharing. Negative emotions in your body can turn into mean words, pushing someone, or other hurtful things, if you act on them.

When we experience an emotion, we feel it inside our body, but we often show it to the outer world with smiles, laughter, or not-so-nice words. And if we pay attention, we can see that other people are always showing us how they feel. Dad may come home from work singing and carrying a large pizza for everyone to share. He's feeling positive. Or Mom might walk in crying because she got a flat tire on the way home from work. She's not feeling so good.

When we spot emotions in other people, it helps us understand emotions more deeply, and it reminds us that we always have a choice in how to handle our emotions.

Of course, the best experience is our own emotions. You may feel happy when you're playing soccer outside on Sunday, but when you need to get up early for school the next morning, you may feel cranky. This is normal, and you have every right to feel your feelings. But—here's the *but*—you are responsible for how you show those emotions. While you can feel cranky, yelling at your family members isn't the best choice.

Learning how you experience different emotions and how they appear in the world can help you make changes if you like.

Copyright © 2022 Maureen Healy. *The Happiness Workbook for Kids.* All rights reserved.

To Do

Positive emotions feel good inside and aren't usually challenging to handle. Match the positive emotion on the left with how you might display it in your world.

Loved	Telling jokes
Joyful	Writing thank-you notes
Grateful	Hugging your family members
Calm	Standing tall and smiling
Silly	Jumping up and down
Confident	Flying a kite
Relaxed	Sleeping in a hammock
Excited	Counting the days until vacation
Kind	Sharing your lunch
Hopeful	Watching the sunset
Brave	Playing a new game for the first time

Did this exercise bring up any good memories of positive emotions? If so, which ones?

_____

_____

_____

_____

_____

Copyright © 2022 Maureen Healy. *The Happiness Workbook for Kids*. All rights reserved.

... And More to Do

Negative emotions don't feel good, and they can be challenging to handle. Oftentimes, when you act out your negative feelings, problems arise for yourself and others. Read through each of the made-up examples below, and then use this list of negative emotions to describe what you would be feeling in that situation:

Angry	Frustrated	Guilty
Sad	Anxious	Misunderstood
Jealous	Lazy	Disgusted
Scared	Hurt	Lonely
Annoyed	Disappointed	Embarrassed

You push someone on the playground. What are you feeling?

_____

You walk into your classroom and accidentally step in gum. What are you feeling?

_____

You cheat on your spelling quiz but wish you hadn't done so afterward. What are you feeling?

_____

You have to get books from the dark closet. What are you feeling?

_____

A new kid in class pronounces your name wrong every day. What are you feeling?

_____

Your best friend gets the brand-new sneakers you wanted. What are you feeling?

_____

You don't want to share your new video game. What are you feeling?

_____

Copyright © 2022 Maureen Healy. *The Happiness Workbook for Kids*. All rights reserved.

Ideas to Remember

We experience our emotions on the inside but show them on the outside. When you feel positive emotions, like enthusiasm, you may hug someone or say nice words to them. But when you're feeling more difficult emotions, like anger, you might say some not-so-nice things or push someone on the playground. The point is to understand what the different emotions look like in the world, since everyone on the planet (including animals) has feelings and expresses them in different ways.

Learning how to spot emotions in yourself and others can help you make smart choices on what to do with them. For example, instead of being mean to someone when you feel angry, you can learn to walk away. Of course, you have a right to feel *all* your feelings. But learning how to safely and smartly express them—even the tricky, tough ones—is our job on the path to happier life experiences.

Copyright © 2022 Maureen Healy. *The Happiness Workbook for Kids.* All rights reserved.

Activity 7

Choices

HAPPINESS LESSON

Paying attention to your emotions (positive and negative) is helpful. It's only when you realize what you're feeling (for example, happy or frustrated) that you can stop and make a smart choice about what to do. Smart choices are good for you and good for others!

You have many emotions. Sometimes you might feel excited and enthusiastic, while other times you might feel disappointed and mad. You probably also feel big emotions sometimes and react quickly in these moments. *Learning how to slow down, stop, and make smart choices with your big feelings is helpful.*

For example, Quinn was playing catch in his living room with his best friend, Toby. While playing, Quinn accidentally missed catching the ball and broke his mother's favorite vase. What should he do?

    A. Tell the truth (and quickly)

    B. Blame Toby

    C. Say he has no idea what happened

    D. Suggest it might have been an earthquake

    E. Apologize for his mistake

All of these choices are possible, but only two are smart. They are A and E, because both of them are good for everyone. Choice B, C, or D would be a lie and potentially hurt someone (Toby, in choice B). Not-so-smart choices often cause problems for you or someone else.

So, Quinn did choose A and E. He wanted to be honest, and he knew those were the only smart choices.

Copyright © 2022 Maureen Healy. *The Happiness Workbook for Kids.* All rights reserved.

To Do

Making a smart choice about how to handle emotions takes practice. Remember, smart choices are good for you and others. Imagine one of your classmates starts "talking trash" with you and says, "You stink at basketball." Instead of shaking it off, you get really annoyed and angry inside.

Circle the smart choices you can make in this situation:

Punch him	Take some time alone
Ignore him	Go hang with other friends
Speak up for yourself	Say, "That's not cool or true"
Start a rumor about him	Tell a teacher
Take a break	Make fun of him
Walk away	Ask him what his problem is
Push him	Ask him to stop
Do some deep breathing	

Remember, smart choices are good for you and good for others. If the choices you circled would not harm you or anyone else—whether in words or actions—you were correct.

Eventually, we want to become more like ducks. Ducks let water roll off their backs, and we can learn to let other people's mean words or actions just roll off us. You can even say "quack, quack" when someone is mean and walk away, which is funny and helpful. Of course, if you ever feel unsafe, it's always a smart choice to ask for help from a caring adult.

... And More to Do

Everyone experiences negative emotions. *Learning how to slow down and stop yourself before making a not-so-smart choice with an emotion takes practice.* The list below includes some ways to slow yourself down and get calmer so you can make the best choice. Circle the ones you might like to use.

Take a deep breath	Talk to a friend
Walk away	Ask for help
Hit a punching bag	Listen to music
Exercise	Play (video games, toys, etc.)
Draw	Read
Keep a journal	Help someone else
Cry	Go outside
Spend time with animals	Take a nap

Is there anything else you can do to help you slow down and feel calmer? If so, please share.

_____

_____

_____

_____

Copyright © 2022 Maureen Healy. *The Happiness Workbook for Kids.* All rights reserved.

Ideas to Remember

It is helpful to learn how to make smart choices with our emotions. *A smart choice is one that's good for you and good for others.* Letting your anger out by screaming may help you find some relief from your anger, but it may also be challenging for others. Instead, a smart choice may be to talk through the problem or walk away until you feel calmer.

Becoming better and better at making smart emotional choices takes time, practice, and an understanding of how emotions work. But it's important since your best life is made up of smart choices. You can do this!

Copyright © 2022 Maureen Healy. *The Happiness Workbook for Kids.* All rights reserved.

Changing Emotions

HAPPINESS LESSON

Emotions are always changing. They are like the weather. Some days are rainy, and other days are sunny. When you learn to let emotions come and go (just like clouds passing by in the sky), you don't let yourself get stuck in any emotion, especially the uncomfortable ones. This is one of the essential lessons on how emotions work.

Sanjay was picked on by his classmates, who said the lunches he brought from home smelled funny. One day, he got angry and threw his lunchbox across the cafeteria. Unfortunately, the lunchbox hit another boy, who needed stitches. This wasn't a smart choice. Sanjay forgot that his feeling of anger would eventually change, and instead he reacted while he was angry (not a good idea). Instead of reacting while he was angry, Sanjay could have let a teacher or another trusted adult know that he was being bullied.

With the help of Sanjay's teacher, his whole class began learning more about emotions and how they work. These lessons helped them make better choices. This is what they learned:

- Emotions change.

- Don't get stuck in one emotion.

- Learn to let emotions come and go.

- You're in charge.

- Pay attention to little feelings.

- Little feelings get bigger, so be careful.

When you remember that emotions are always changing, you won't be fooled by the temporary "rainy weather." Instead, you'll remember that inside of you there is goodness and sunshine. Of course, it doesn't mean things will always be easy, but with practice you can learn how to let big and challenging emotions visit and then let them go smartly.

Copyright © 2022 Maureen Healy. *The Happiness Workbook for Kids*. All rights reserved.

To Do

A young girl asked her grandfather about emotions. This girl was very excited to hear what her grandfather had to say because he was often happy and seemed to have so many things figured out. What he said to his dear granddaughter is the following:

> Emotions are like clouds. They come and go. Never hold on to emotions, whether it's joy or sadness. Let them pass by like a cloud. Just watch them go by. You are like the sunny sky behind the clouds. You are always there, but sometimes stormy clouds come in front of you and it's hard to see the sunshine. But the more you let the clouds float by, the more you can get in touch with your natural self, which is good and positive.

Smiling, the young girl thanked her grandfather and went to go think. She sat outside and watched the clouds, and she noticed how they are always moving, just like her emotions.

One theme of this story is to not get stuck in your emotions, but to let them float away like clouds in the sky. Do you ever get stuck in your emotions? If so, which ones?

_____

_____

Read through the following actions, and circle the ones you think would help you get unstuck from a negative emotion (like frustration or anger) and help you feel a bit better.

Ask for help	Take a walk	Sit outside
Say, "Let it go"	Talk to someone	Go watch the clouds
Write in a journal	Squeeze a stress ball	Pet your dog
Draw it out	Take five deep breaths	Listen to music

Copyright © 2022 Maureen Healy. *The Happiness Workbook for Kids.* All rights reserved.

... And More to Do

Determine if the following statements are true or false.

Anger is one of the most challenging emotions.

_____True   _____False

Children can get stuck in sadness.

_____True   _____False

Emotions can float away like clouds if we let them.

_____True   _____False

Hitting someone is a not-so-smart choice.

_____True   _____False

You can learn to think a new thought and get a new feeling.

_____True   _____False

Learning to smartly manage tough emotions takes practice.

_____True   _____False

Your body sends you signs about how you feel.

_____True   _____False

Paying attention to your emotions is important.

_____True   _____False

If you answered *true* for all of these statements, you are 100 percent correct. If not, let's remember you're learning, and that's a good thing!

Copyright © 2022 Maureen Healy. *The Happiness Workbook for Kids.* All rights reserved.

Ideas to Remember

Emotions are temporary. And you can learn how to let emotions come and go, like clouds floating away in the sky. Of course, some emotions are harder than others. But when you remember that emotions don't last forever, this can give you strength, especially if you're faced with a challenging emotion like anger, sadness, or frustration.

Understanding more about how emotions work, which includes seeing them as temporary, is an important step on the path to becoming happier.

Copyright © 2022 Maureen Healy. *The Happiness Workbook for Kids.* All rights reserved.

2

Expressing Emotions

· · · · · · · · · · · ·

Being able to express your emotions in a healthy way is something you learn. When you first learned to swim, or ride a bike, or read, you probably had another person to guide you. It's the same with feelings: In order to learn how to effectively manage your emotions, you need a teacher, friend, or book like this to help you. In this section, you will learn how to slow down your fast-moving emotions. That way, you can stop and make smart choices, even when things feel hard.

Activity 9

You're the Captain

Emotions can arrive fast and feel big. Learning that you are bigger than your emotions can help you remember that *you're* in charge, not your emotions. You are the captain, and you are steering your "emotional boat" wherever you choose.

Imagine each of us has a boat. It's an invisible emotional boat. Only you can steer your emotional boat, whether it's in bumpy waters (like anger, sadness, or fear) or calmer waters (like hope, interest, or joy). Since you are the captain of your emotional boat, you'll need to learn how to:

- Slow down or speed up

- Stop (put down the invisible anchor)

- Turn your boat around

- Enjoy the ride

There might come a moment when you feel you are going in the "wrong" emotional direction, in which case you can then slow down, stop, and turn your boat in a better-feeling direction. Sometimes it's easy to change directions, and other times it takes much longer. That's okay; there's no rush.

Of course, it's also okay to want to put your anchor down so you can stop and enjoy the happier moments in life. And it's also okay to want to move through challenges quickly. But the goal isn't to avoid challenges—it's to learn how to sail skillfully through any weather and toward your own happier moments.

Copyright © 2022 Maureen Healy. *The Happiness Workbook for Kids*. All rights reserved.

To Do

You're a powerful captain. You can learn to use your power to move toward sunnier and happier days and to move through challenges smartly. The first step is to believe you can. It happens with your thoughts and actions.

Inside the frame, tape a photo or draw a picture of yourself. Make a list around the frame of ways you've already used your power to learn something new or do something challenging. For example, David just got his yellow belt in karate, Mischa is learning how to speak Mandarin, and Chris finished putting together a 500-piece puzzle of outer space.

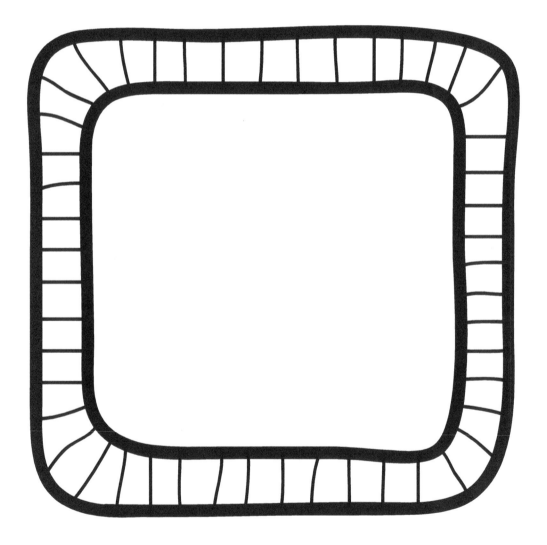

Copyright © 2022 Maureen Healy. *The Happiness Workbook for Kids*. All rights reserved.

... And More to Do

Realizing that you've already used your power to learn new things and share your talents can help you feel confident. The list at the bottom of the page includes some words that describe how powerful you are today. Use the word bank here to fill in the blanks:

Capable	Valuable
Powerful	Safe
Strong	Loved
Smart	Talented
Worthy	Amazing

_ O R T _ Y   _ M _ R _

L _ _ E D   T _ L _ N _ _ D

_ A _ E   P O _ _ R _ U _

S _ _ O N G   A _ _ Z _ N G

V _ L _ _ B L E   _ A P _ _ L _

Copyright © 2022 Maureen Healy. *The Happiness Workbook for Kids*. All rights reserved.

Ideas to Remember

Only you can feel your feelings and make choices on what to do with them. It's important to remember that feelings are temporary (they don't last forever) and that you're bigger than your biggest feeling. When you understand more about how emotions work, you can learn how to safely express them as the captain of your emotional ship.

The point isn't to avoid your emotions, but to learn how to sail through them—no matter what they are—and move toward better-feeling experiences and emotions.

Copyright © 2022 Maureen Healy. *The Happiness Workbook for Kids*. All rights reserved.

Activity 10

Paying Attention

HAPPINESS LESSON

The weather is always changing, just like us. There are sunny days, foggy ones, and even snow days (the best kind). Learning how to slow down and pay attention to the weather outside—and inside of you—takes practice. The more you pay attention, the better choices you can make.

A lot of kids like to go fast—they want to fill each day with as many fun things as possible! Some kids even feel like they *have* to go fast. They have a lot to do (like homework, after-school activities, and chores) before they can relax. But the more you learn to *slow down* and really see what is happening around you, the better choices you can make. Let's do an experiment to see how much of life you are seeing right now. Raise your hand if:

- You are wearing blue

- Your name begins with an M

- You have a pet (at home)

- You can see the sky

Whether you raised your hand or not, this short activity encouraged you to pay closer attention to details (for example, what colors you are wearing). The more you pay attention to the world around you, the more you see.

We can also learn to pay more attention to ourselves—our bodies, thoughts, and feelings—so we can make the best choices. Remember your emotional boat? Paying close attention helps you steer your boat successfully so you don't sink!

Copyright © 2022 Maureen Healy. *The Happiness Workbook for Kids*. All rights reserved.

To Do

Look at these two pictures. What is different between picture A and picture B? Take your time and look carefully. Circle any differences you find.

Picture A

Picture B

Copyright © 2022 Maureen Healy. *The Happiness Workbook for Kids*. All rights reserved.

... And More to Do

Learning how to pay attention takes practice. Think of something you love. It's probably easy to pay attention because you care so much about this thing. *You can learn to bring this same kind of focus to other things in life, especially your emotions.*

Let's begin to pay attention on purpose *right now* as you answer the following questions.

Look around you. What do you see that's red?

_____

_____

_____

_____

Look around again. What do you see that's white?

_____

_____

_____

_____

Now put on your "elephant ears" so you can listen more closely. Close your eyes, and listen to the sounds around you for a full minute. What did you hear?

_____

_____

_____

_____

Can paying attention help in other parts of your life? Tell me about a situation or place where paying attention can really help you (video games count too!).

_____

_____

_____

_____

Copyright © 2022 Maureen Healy. *The Happiness Workbook for Kids.* All rights reserved.

Ideas to Remember

Slowing down and paying attention helps us become better captains. We can slow down our emotional boat and go in a new direction if we need to. The purpose of paying attention isn't to avoid the problems of life (like worry, fear, sadness, and disappointment) but to sail through them more easily and learn how to create positive experiences (like joy, gratitude, hope, and happiness).

Copyright © 2022 Maureen Healy. *The Happiness Workbook for Kids*. All rights reserved.

Smart Choices Checklist

HAPPINESS LESSON

We are always making choices. Sometimes we make not-so-smart choices, and that's part of life. But we can often begin again. Smart choices are good for you and good for others. They help move us toward our happier life experiences. Using a "smart choices checklist" can help us make these good decisions in the classroom, at home, or anywhere else!

Choices are everywhere. What socks will I wear today? What will I eat for lunch? Will I play video games or do my homework? Life is full of choices, and some choices will move you toward happier life experiences, while others will move you away. *Remember that smart choices are good for you and good for others.* They help you move toward better experiences.

You probably know some people (including adults!) who don't always make smart choices. They are learning too. The way you know you made a smart choice is when your choice is good for you and good for others. But making the right choice isn't always easy.

For example, Piper was at lacrosse practice, and she was excited for the game that day. She ran out onto the field and her teammate, Hailey, called her "four-eyes" because of her new glasses. Piper quickly got angry. She wanted to hit Hailey with her lacrosse stick, and she started walking toward her—but then she remembered what she had learned about smart choices. Piper stopped, took a deep breath, and walked away.

Learning how to pay attention, stop ourselves, and make smart choices is the homework of a happier life. Piper wanted to hit Hailey, but she decided to make a smart choice instead.

Copyright © 2022 Maureen Healy. *The Happiness Workbook for Kids.* All rights reserved.

To Do

After school, Mike was playing his favorite video game, and he was almost done leveling up. His mom came into the room and said, "Turn off the game!" But Mike didn't even hear his mom since he was so focused on the game. After a few minutes, his mom came back into the room and said, "Turn off the game, or you will get your screen taken away for a week!" Mike heard his mom this time.

Circle the correct answer to each question.

At the beginning of the story, Mike was playing:

A video game   Hide-and-seek   Follow-the-leader

Mike's mom got frustrated and told Mike he would get his _____ taken away.

Dinner   Screen   Homework

At the end of the story, Mike has a choice on how to respond to his mom. A *not-so-smart choice* would be:

Smile   Walk away   Scream

A *smart choice* that Mike could make would be to:

Put the screen away   Throw the screen   Stomp and scream

A lot of kids enjoy "screen time"—playing video games, watching movies, and more. When your screen time is over, is it easy for you to stop? Or is it hard sometimes? If it's hard, what could make it easier?

_____

_____

_____

_____

Copyright © 2022 Maureen Healy. *The Happiness Workbook for Kids*. All rights reserved.

... And More to Do

Smart choices are good for you and good for others. For example, you may want to scream when you're angry, but that's not good for others. That isn't a smart choice. A better choice might be to talk it out or walk away. Complete the following sentences by describing a smart choice you could make in each situation.

Your brother broke your toy. You want to scream. Instead you:

_____

_____

_____

You're painting, and you spill paint all over your favorite shorts. You want to throw something. Instead you:

_____

_____

_____

You had a surprise spelling quiz today, and you got 25 percent correct. You want to kick something. Instead you:

_____

_____

_____

At recess, someone pushes you. You want to push them back. Instead you:

_____

_____

_____

Smart choices take practice. We may not make smart choices every time (in fact, we probably won't), but the more we practice paying attention and choosing smartly, the better we will get at handling our emotions.

Copyright © 2022 Maureen Healy. *The Happiness Workbook for Kids.* All rights reserved.

... And a Bonus To-Do!

Before you begin a sailing trip, you decide where you want to go, and you look at a map to figure out how to get there. You do the same thing when you want to feel good. You can use a "smart choices checklist" to figure out what things you can do or think to help yourself feel better when big emotions pop up. That way, if you face any choppy waters along the way—such as anger, fear, worry, or sadness—you already have a list of ideas that will help you turn your boat around.

Smart Choices Checklist

List three things you can do or think **at home** to help you feel better when a big emotion comes to visit. Remember, emotions are only temporary visitors.

1. _____

2. _____

3. _____

List three things you can do or think **at school** to help you feel better when a big emotion comes to visit.

1. _____

2. _____

3. _____

Finally, list three things you can do or think **anywhere**—wherever you happen to be—to help you feel better when a big emotion comes to visit.

1. _____

2. _____

3. _____

When your emotional boat is going through rough seas, it's helpful to understand what calms you down and guides you into calmer waters. Think of it like an emotional map to help you steer your boat—and not crash into any icebergs!

Copyright © 2022 Maureen Healy. *The Happiness Workbook for Kids*. All rights reserved.

Ideas to Remember

Smart choices are good for you and good for others. *Using a smart choices checklist can help you make better choices*—even when you're experiencing a challenging emotion, like anger.

Learning how to slow down, take a beat (breathe, pause), and then make a smarter choice takes practice. You can probably think of plenty of people (adults included) who are still learning how to make smart choices. With time and practice, smart choices become easier and easier to make, especially if you read books like this or have people in your life who can teach you how.

Copyright © 2022 Maureen Healy. *The Happiness Workbook for Kids*. All rights reserved.

Activity 12

Negative Emotions

Emotions point to how we're feeling inside. Negative emotions are often challenging, but they are a natural part of life. Some common negative emotions are anger, sadness, disappointment, and loneliness. Learning how to steer our emotional boats through these feelings helps us become the best captains we can be.

Challenging emotions are not bad. *There are no bad emotions.* Emotions are simply sending us signs about how we are feeling inside at any given time. It may be a joyful time (positive emotion) or a sad time (negative emotion). When we say *negative* emotion, it means *more challenging*, since it can be harder to feel calm and make smart choices.

Of course, you're encouraged to feel all your feelings, from hope and excitement to anger and sadness. There's no problem with feeling any of these feelings, but ultimately, you need to learn how to handle the challenging emotions skillfully and make those smart choices.

For example, the emotion of sadness might make you feel like there is a cloud over your head and like you cannot escape. You feel stuck and powerless. But the truth is, that feeling will pass. Sadness is considered a negative emotion—not because it's bad, but simply because it can be tricky to remember to ask for help from others, or to let it pass, before making a not-so-smart choice.

Becoming the best captain you can be includes learning how to smartly handle negative (challenging, tricky) emotions, as well as positive (helpful) emotions.

Copyright © 2022 Maureen Healy. *The Happiness Workbook for Kids.* All rights reserved.

To Do

Challenging emotions aren't bad emotions. They simply aren't the easiest emotions to handle. But remember: *You are* bigger *than even your biggest emotions, and you can safely express them.* The first step is to name your emotions.

Draw a line from the emotion in the left column to its definition (meaning) in the right column.

Sadness	The feeling of disapproval and yuckiness
Worry	The feeling of wanting what someone else has
Anger	The feeling of concern and nervousness
Frustration	The feeling of too many things at once
Jealousy	The feeling of not liking how things are
Disgust	The feeling of intense frustration (feeling mad)
Overwhelm	The feeling of being unhappy

Copyright © 2022 Maureen Healy. *The Happiness Workbook for Kids.* All rights reserved.

... And More to Do

Our negative emotions (rainy days) balance our positive emotions (sunny days). The point isn't to have all happy days, but to understand that almost any day can become better. You are learning how to sail through life regardless of the weather and how to move toward your best experiences.

Let's examine three challenging emotions more deeply:

Worry　　When you're worried, you feel nervous about something happening. You can worry about something you are afraid will happen in the future or worry about something from the past that you're afraid will happen again. Coming back to the present moment—to what is happening *right now*—can help calm the worry storm. For example, you can do breathing exercises or an activity that takes focus, like shooting hoops.

Sadness　　When you're sad, you feel unhappy. You might have lost something or had your feelings hurt. Sadness gets better if we talk to other people, use our creativity, and move our bodies. Sometimes children need help from adults and doctors to feel better too. Sadness can get worse if we don't connect with our loved ones, like our friends, family, and pets.

Anger　　When you're angry, you may feel very frustrated and disappointed. You may have gotten a lousy grade, or someone said something mean to you. Whatever got you angry, you don't feel good. It helps to remember that anger is only visiting you temporarily—let it come in, and let it go (without harm to anyone). You may want to do something to let the anger go, like hit a punching bag, go for a walk, or talk to someone.

Every challenging emotion has a strategy you can use to help reduce it. Learning how to work with your emotions takes practice. The good news is, the more you practice, the healthier and happier you can become.

Copyright © 2022 Maureen Healy. *The Happiness Workbook for Kids*. All rights reserved.

Let's consider those three emotions again, and identify one thing that can help you reduce or express each of them smartly. (Refer to the previous page for hints.)

Worry feels like a storm. How can you calm the storm and return your focus to the present moment?

_____

_____

_____

_____

Sadness is heavy. It makes you want to cry and be alone. What can you do or think differently to feel a little bit better?

_____

_____

_____

_____

Anger is fast and feels big. How can you handle your anger smartly?

_____

_____

_____

_____

Copyright © 2022 Maureen Healy. *The Happiness Workbook for Kids*. All rights reserved.

Ideas to Remember

Challenging emotions aren't easy. But you are bigger than even your BIGGEST feeling, and you can learn to send it on its way (most of the time). Of course, there are some days that are simply rainy days. They will pass. *Your job is to learn how emotions work and to then make smart choices with them.*

Remember, your job isn't to be perfect (that's impossible!). The only expectation is that you do your best, and when you make a mistake—like we all do—you learn from it and move on.

Your happier life experiences await you!

Copyright © 2022 Maureen Healy. *The Happiness Workbook for Kids.* All rights reserved.

Creating Calm

HAPPINESS LESSON

When we're feeling big emotions, using strategies like breathing exercises or jumping on a trampoline can help us feel calmer. When we have a calm mind, we can make the smartest choices even with the biggest emotions. Calming ourselves takes practice, but it allows us to more easily steer our emotional boat toward better-feeling experiences!

Imagine you are steering your emotional boat. There are rough waters ahead, and you can see the shore. Of course, the problem is that you must steer through the big waves, windy skies, and rain coming down. You need a calm mind that can focus on the landing ahead and not become troubled by the stormy weather.

The same is true for your big emotions. When you feel calm, it's easier to make a smart choice (one that's good for you and good for others). But when you feel completely stormy, it becomes extremely difficult to see clearly and to make it neatly to the other side of that big emotion.

Learning a few calming tools to include in your captain's toolbox can help you steer your boat, especially when the waves are big and your emotions run high.

Copyright © 2022 Maureen Healy. *The Happiness Workbook for Kids.* All rights reserved.

To Do

Calming our bodies and minds takes practice. One way to calm ourselves is to take deep breaths. This helps our bodies feel emotionally balanced (instead of feeling off-balance). There are many different types of breathing exercises, but some of my favorite ones are listed here. Try each of them.

Flower Breath

Imagine you are holding a flower in your hand, and blow off all the petals. Take a deep breath in through your nose, then blow the air out through your mouth. Repeat three times.

Hot Soup Breath

Imagine there's a bowl of hot soup in front of you. To make it cooler, blow on it. Take a deep breath in through your nose, then blow the air out through your mouth. Repeat five times.

Five for Five

Hold out your hand, and make a fist. Take a deep breath in through your nose and out through your mouth. Pop out one finger from your fist after each breath, and repeat four times until your fist is open.

Hand on Heart

Place one hand on your heart and feel your heart beating. Take a deep breath in through your nose and out through your mouth. Feel your body begin to feel calmer. Repeat for ten breaths.

Copyright © 2022 Maureen Healy. *The Happiness Workbook for Kids.* All rights reserved.

... And More to Do

Breathing activities can calm the body and mind. Of course, they are not the only way to slow us down, calm our bodies, and help us make better choices. Here are some more ideas:

- Take a walk
- Pet a dog or cat
- Hit a punching bag
- Jump on a trampoline
- Talk to someone
- Close your eyes (for a few minutes)
- Play a video game
- Exercise (basketball, jump rope, etc.)
- Read a good book
- Count to 100
- Take a nap

- Sing a song
- Squeeze a stress ball
- Use a fidget spinner
- Draw it out
- Get a hug
- Take a break
- Do ten jumping jacks
- Do yoga
- Listen to a bedtime story
- Repeat a calming word, like "peace"
- Do another activity you love

Fill in each of the following sentences using one of the activities listed (or something else you can think of that will help you).

Someone says something mean to you. You get angry. To feel calmer, you:

_____

You forgot your lunch and your homework. This is a very bad, miserable day. To feel better, you decide to:

_____

You feel 100 percent bored in history class. You want to scream, but instead, to feel calmer, you decide to:

_____

Copyright © 2022 Maureen Healy. *The Happiness Workbook for Kids*. All rights reserved.

Ideas to Remember

Calming ourselves gets easier with practice. Some of the common ways to calm ourselves include using breathing activities and doing something physical to let the not-so-calm feelings out.

There are many other activities you can use too—the list is endless! The important point is that you find something that helps you calm down and that stops you from making a not-so-smart choice.

Copyright © 2022 Maureen Healy. *The Happiness Workbook for Kids.* All rights reserved.

Activity 14

Positive Emotions

HAPPINESS LESSON

Inside of you (at the center) is the positive emotion of peace (feeling calm). Other positive emotions you can have include hope, love, gratitude, and enthusiasm. Positive emotions feel good and benefit yourself, as well as others. You can learn how to create positive emotions through your thoughts and actions in the world.

Steering your emotional boat through calm waters feels good. The sun is shining, and the wind is at your back. All is well. You don't have a worry in the world. Of course, we all want to feel good and have days like this. The question is: What can you do to feel good more often?

Well, there's lots you can do! You can create positive emotions through your thoughts and your actions (most of the time). When you're steering your emotional boat, you might hit rough waters or feel like you're sinking—but you can learn to stop, calm yourself, and then move in a better-feeling direction. Instead of being a Debbie Downer (negative person) you could say, "I've got this" and "We're on our way to a better day!"

Of course, the goal isn't to always feel happy, but to sail your way skillfully through stormy and sunny times as you move toward becoming the best emotional captain you can be!

Copyright © 2022 Maureen Healy. *The Happiness Workbook for Kids*. All rights reserved.

To Do

Increasing positive emotions takes practice (and patience, another positive emotion!). Some positive emotions are listed below.

Draw a line from the emotion in the left column to its definition (meaning) in the right column.

Relief	The feeling of thankfulness
Gratitude	The feeling of peace and quiet
Confidence	The feeling of stress going away
Enthusiasm	The feeling that you can do it
Calmness	The feeling of excitement
Self-love	The feeling of loving yourself
Silliness	The feeling of happiness
Joy	The feeling of being goofy and funny

Tell me about something you do or think that helps you feel one of these positive emotions. You might tell me about the last time you felt silly or joyful.

_____

_____

_____

Copyright © 2022 Maureen Healy. *The Happiness Workbook for Kids*. All rights reserved.

... And More to Do

You can also create positive emotions by saying affirmations, which are positive, feel-good sayings that you believe about yourself (or that you'll believe soon). The act of saying them aloud is powerful, but even thinking certain affirmations or mottos can improve your mood and help you feel more positive.

For example, Emily felt afraid whenever she had to cross over the Golden Gate Bridge on her way to school. At first, she said, "I can't do this" and she'd feel even more afraid. But she soon learned how to say, "I am safe" and "All is well" as she crossed the bridge in her family's car. Before long, Emily felt calmer and safer as she crossed the bridge, which moved her to a more positive feeling.

So, as you can imagine, there are all different types of affirmations. Some include:

This is a happy day!

All is well.

I'm an amazing person!

I'm getting better and better at _____.

I am always in the right place, at the right time.

I am peaceful (feeling calm).

I'm perfect just as I am!

Now that you understand what an affirmation is, let's have you create some "I am..." affirmations. Fill in the following lines with some feel-good affirmations about yourself. You might say, "I am happy" or "I'm loved" or "I'm a great artist!"

I am _____.

I am _____.

I am _____.

I am _____.

Copyright © 2022 Maureen Healy. *The Happiness Workbook for Kids*. All rights reserved.

... And a Bonus To-Do!

Think back to the last time you were feeling really good, and create your own personal comic strip of that experience. For example, you might remember opening gifts on your birthday or bicycling with your friends.

Remember: The more you focus on the good things in life, the more positive feelings you'll experience on a regular basis.

Title: _____

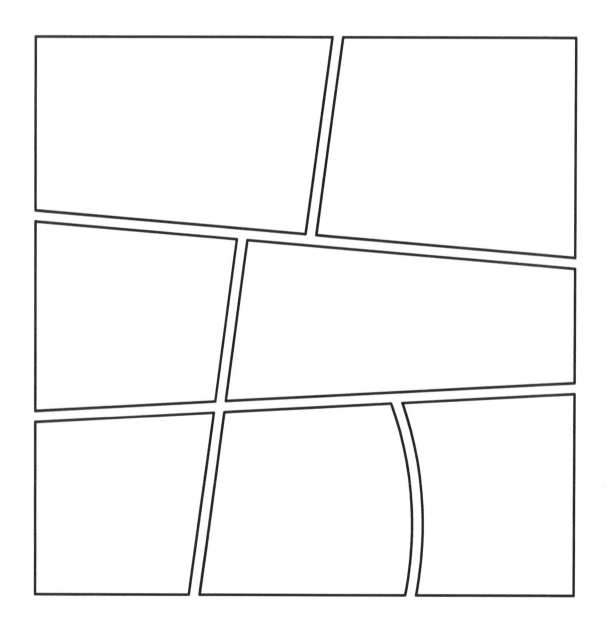

Copyright © 2022 Maureen Healy. *The Happiness Workbook for Kids*. All rights reserved.

Ideas to Remember

You are the captain of your emotional boat. You can steer your boat toward or away from positive emotions—it's up to you. Only you can feel your feelings and think (or do) something different to feel better.

Putting tools into your captain's toolbox can help you when the weather feels stormy or cloudy. For example, you might say affirmations or mottos like "a sunny day is coming my way" or use a breathing exercise. You can also choose to focus on—and be thankful for—all the positive things in your life.

Copyright © 2022 Maureen Healy. *The Happiness Workbook for Kids*. All rights reserved.

Activity 15

Three Steps

HAPPINESS LESSON

Captains don't learn to sail in one day! They go to sailing school, take practice trips, learn about the instruments, and follow specific directions that take them safely to shore. The same is true when it comes to managing our emotions. The "three steps" is a strategy we practice over and over because it takes us safely to a better-feeling place.

Steering your emotional boat toward sunnier and happier days takes practice. The "three steps" to success are easy to remember (but tougher to do), and following them will help you feel better faster. The three steps are:

1. Stop.

2. Calm (and center) yourself.

3. Make a smart choice.

Catching ourselves and stopping before we make a not-so-smart choice takes practice. For example, Liam recently got in trouble for pushing his classmate Archie during recess. Liam doesn't normally act this way, but Archie was teasing him, and Liam became so angry that he acted without thinking. He missed step 1.

But with time, and a few talks with the school counselor, Liam learned how to slow down and stop before acting on his anger. Archie still teases him sometimes, but Liam takes deep breaths and walks away. He can now remember step 1 (stop) and step 2 (calm) so he can get to step 3 (smart choice).

Whether you have challenges with anger or another emotion, using these three steps to success can help you slow down and make a better-feeling choice.

Copyright © 2022 Maureen Healy. *The Happiness Workbook for Kids*. All rights reserved.

To Do

Ollie is the star soccer player on his team. He loves to be outside and kick the ball into the net. He can easily master new skills on the soccer field, but he finds it harder to learn new things in school and do his homework, which makes him feel annoyed. Ollie gets particularly frustrated with math, which usually ends up with him throwing his books, homework sheets, and pencils across the room. You could say he gets "hot" with anger.

Can Ollie learn the three steps (stop, calm, make a smarter choice) and do things better?

Yes   Maybe   No

Do you think Ollie feels anger signals in his body?

Yes   Maybe   No

Is Ollie catching his anger signals? In other words, is he stopping himself before making a not-so-smart choice?

Yes   Maybe   No

Do you ever feel like Ollie and get frustrated or angry?

Yes   Maybe   No

What helps you catch your anger signals when they're small?

_____

_____

_____

... And More to Do

Think back to a time when you were on the stormy seas of life and felt a really big, challenging emotion (like anger, sadness, loss, or worry). Can you remember what you did in that situation that helped you feel calmer? Did you take a deep breath, squeeze your stress ball, or go for a walk? Or maybe you did something else.

In the frame, draw a picture of what you did to feel calmer. If you simply thought of something new, draw or write the thought that helped you feel better.

Copyright © 2022 Maureen Healy. *The Happiness Workbook for Kids*. All rights reserved.

... And a Bonus To-Do!

Making smart choices isn't about being perfect (that's impossible), but it does mean you are learning to do things that are good for you and good for others. The sooner you identify what a smart choice looks and feels like, the easier it is to make that smart choice.

Name three smart choices that help you feel better and move you in a good direction, especially when you're feeling a big and challenging emotion. You might say, "Go for a walk" or "Ask for a break" as two examples.

1 _____

2 _____

3 _____

Copyright © 2022 Maureen Healy. *The Happiness Workbook for Kids.* All rights reserved.

Ideas to Remember

Being able to steer your emotional boat in any direction takes practice, which includes learning how to steer through the big waves of life (feelings). Of course, there are days that feel sunny and good without any problems, but other days feel cloudy and more challenging.

Remembering the three steps we just learned can help you move in a better-feeling direction no matter what is happening. Again, they are:

1. **Stop** and catch yourself—slow down and take a beat.

2. **Calm** and center yourself using the strategies you've learned.

3. **Make a smart choice:** one that's good for you and good for others.

Copyright © 2022 Maureen Healy. *The Happiness Workbook for Kids*. All rights reserved.

Begin Again

HAPPINESS LESSON

Becoming the best captain often requires some "do-overs" on the way. These are the moments when you're steering your boat, but you accidentally run into stormy weather (big feelings) and make a not-so-smart choice (it happens to all of us!). The good news is that you can usually begin again or start over.

Everyone on the planet is learning. This includes your family members, teachers, and friends. As we learn, we do some things well—but other times, we need do-overs. After all, no one is perfect! Starting over can be challenging if we've made a really big mistake, but other times we simply need to let it go or shake it off.

Think about the last time you wanted a do-over. It might have been on the basketball court when you were learning how to block someone. Maybe you went too far and bumped them onto the floor. You got fouled and had to start again. Or maybe you were upset with a classmate and needed a friendship do-over. Or perhaps you did poorly on an assignment and asked the teacher if you could redo it.

We all have big feelings and make mistakes sometimes. Some of them are small, and others are a little bigger. The opportunity to begin again, and get another chance to get it right, is helpful. Because with practice, you can become a really skilled emotional captain who creates happier life experiences.

Copyright © 2022 Maureen Healy. *The Happiness Workbook for Kids*. All rights reserved.

To Do

Starting over can be a smart choice. It gives you more time to practice and to do your best. Read through the situations below, and circle any situation where someone might want to try again.

Throwing a basketball and missing the hoop

Falling down the slope while skiing

Singing off-key

Sending a not-so-nice text

Oversleeping and missing the bus

Knocking over a classmate's project on purpose

Making terrible pancakes

Losing a video game

If you circled any of these situations, you are correct. They are all opportunities that someone may want to do over. With a little practice, we get better and move toward—not away—from feeling and doing our best.

Copyright © 2022 Maureen Healy. *The Happiness Workbook for Kids*. All rights reserved.

... And More to Do

Use words or pictures to describe the last time you started over again. Some examples include practicing a solo for your school concert, apologizing to someone, or getting up after falling off your skateboard. There are no wrong answers.

When we feel big emotions, we sometimes make not-so-smart choices. Instead of talking out a problem, maybe we slam the door or say something mean. We react (meaning we do something without thinking)—but with practice, we can learn to slow down and do better.

Read the following items, and put a check mark by the ones that have helped you slow down and start over again.

_____ Listen to music   _____ Walk away   _____ Exercise

_____ Ask for a hug   _____ Talk it out   _____ Take a break

_____ Take deep breaths   _____ Take a nap   _____ Sit alone

_____ Cry   _____ Ask for help   _____ Go outside

Copyright © 2022 Maureen Healy. *The Happiness Workbook for Kids.* All rights reserved.

... And a Bonus To-Do!

Part of growing up involves learning how to ask for what you need, whether it's a glass of water or a do-over with an important person in your life.

Here are some things you might say to another person that might help you start over:

- I'm sorry. Let's start again, okay?

- I need a do-over. Can we start over?

- Can we try that again?

What are some other ways that you could ask for a do-over?

_____

_____

_____

_____

_____

Do you need any do-overs with anyone (like family, friends, or classmates) right now?

_____

_____

_____

_____

_____

Copyright © 2022 Maureen Healy. *The Happiness Workbook for Kids*. All rights reserved.

Ideas to Remember

Emotional do-overs are a normal part of life. They mean you want to do better, and you realize you can do better. This is the gift of beginning again. At any moment, you can begin again. You can take a deep breath and start all over again. The past is gone, and in this present moment, you can start over.

Copyright © 2022 Maureen Healy. *The Happiness Workbook for Kids.* All rights reserved.

3

Becoming Happier

• • • • • • • • • • • •

Becoming happier is a skill you can learn, just like any other skill, such as learning how to ride a bicycle or how to speak another language. Some people have an easier time seeing the bright side of life, but anyone can learn how to become happier with practice. In this section, you will learn what ideas and actions create happier life experiences today—and in the future!

What Is Happier?

HAPPINESS LESSON

We all want to become happier. But what does that mean? *Happier is when your feelings become more positive.* For example, imagine you're learning to play ping pong. You start out and think, "I stink at this." You feel terrible. But you practice some more, and then you think, "Wow, I'm getting better." You feel hopeful. You became happier too.

Happier happens all the time. It can be when you watch your favorite TV show or when you help plan your family's vacation to the Grand Canyon. It is the little and big moments where you *feel better than before.* Your mood improves—and the neat thing is, this can happen no matter how you were feeling before. Maybe you were feeling good, and now you feel great! Or maybe you were feeling angry, and now you feel just a little annoyed; that's also an improvement!

Feeling happier can happen when challenging things go away too. Maybe your teacher cancels the math test. Yay! Or the mean bully moves away, and no one picks on you. What a relief! Any thought or feeling that moves you in a more positive direction can help you become happier.

Sometimes becoming happier is complex too. Here are some additional things that can help move you in a happier direction:

- Helping others

- Thinking about challenges differently

- Using your unique talents

- Making friends

Shortly, we'll discuss these other ways of feeling good and becoming happier too. But let's not forget—becoming happier relies heavily on your skills as the captain of your emotional boat. The better you feel, the better you do.

Copyright © 2022 Maureen Healy. *The Happiness Workbook for Kids.* All rights reserved.

To Do

Happier means you are moving your thoughts and feelings in a more positive direction. You might go from feeling sad to feeling hopeful. This is an improvement. You may not feel happy, exactly, but you are becoming happier—better than before. So, *when you feel happier, you are feeling an improvement in your mood.*

Almost everyone on the planet has a "happy place" where they go because it helps them feel happier. It may be playing in the waves at the beach or sitting in your beanbag chair reading your favorite book. Doing something you enjoy or thinking something positive can also help you become happier.

Complete the following sentences to describe your happy place. There are no wrong answers.

My happy place is _____

In my happy place, I love to _____

_____

_____

My happy person (or pet) is _____

Other happy things I do are _____

_____

_____

_____

_____

Copyright © 2022 Maureen Healy. *The Happiness Workbook for Kids.* All rights reserved.

... And More to Do

Some thoughts help us become happier, while others create more feelings of unhappiness. Choosing thoughts that move you in a happier direction is a skill you can learn. Read through the following situations, and circle the happier thoughts. (Each situation can have more than one happy thought!)

A. Rory's house was damaged in a serious hurricane. He needs to move into temporary housing with his parents while their house is repaired. Rory is stressed about this move and about not having any of his clothes to wear. What happier thoughts can he think?

    1. I have nothing to wear.
    2. It will be fun to buy or borrow different clothes and change it up.
    3. I'm so happy to be alive and okay!

B. Josie's mom is going to the hospital for an operation. The doctors all say that she'll make a full recovery, but Josie is scared. What happier thoughts can she think?

    1. Mom's doctors are the best in the world.
    2. I hate hospitals.
    3. After the surgery, Mom will feel better (and so will I).

C. Maya was walking to the lunch table and tripped. Her lunch tray flew into the air, and food landed everywhere. Feeling embarrassed, she ran out of the cafeteria. What happier thoughts can she think?

    1. That was so embarrassing!
    2. We all drop things. It's normal.
    3. It was a little funny, I bet.

Copyright © 2022 Maureen Healy. *The Happiness Workbook for Kids.* All rights reserved.

Ideas to Remember

You can become happier by choosing thoughts and actions that move you toward more positive feelings. Once you learn how to steer your emotional boat, happiness happens more easily. You can see the sun more often, and when there are clouds (which happen naturally) you move through them. You remember not to put an anchor down in a thunderstorm, but keep moving.

So when there are challenging moments (like sadness, anger, worry, or stress), you can remember they're just temporary, like the weather—and if you do or think something constructive, you can get through those moments and keep moving toward happier life experiences (like hope, gratitude, relief, and joy).

 Copyright © 2022 Maureen Healy. *The Happiness Workbook for Kids*. All rights reserved.

Gratitude

HAPPINESS LESSON

Gratitude moves us toward happier experiences, every single time. We may be feeling angry, sad, or disappointed, but if we can find something—anything—to be grateful for, our mood improves. Happier experiences can happen.

Gratitude helps us become happier. Of course, there are moments when we feel like things aren't going our way. Maybe you step in dog doo-doo or forget to bring your homework to school for the 100th time. You may even say it's a bad day. But even on no-good, rotten days, you can likely find something to feel thankful about, such as:

- You're listening to the birds chirp outside.

- The sun is shining.

- You get to play basketball today.

Gratitude helps you focus on the good things—the things that, even on challenging days, help you feel thankful. The more thankful you can feel even when things are challenging, the easier it is to turn your emotional boat around and sail through the choppy waters of life.

Copyright © 2022 Maureen Healy. *The Happiness Workbook for Kids.* All rights reserved.

To Do

Gratitude is the feeling of being thankful. It's not saying "thank you" without thinking—it's really experiencing the feeling. Gratitude is the recognition that even on days that aren't perfect, there are people, places, and things that you are deeply thankful for (don't forget yourself).

List five things that you're grateful for in this moment:

1. _____

2. _____

3. _____

4. _____

5. _____

Showing your gratitude is called appreciation. If you have ever written a thank-you note, you have appreciated someone else and what they have done for you or given to you. Here are some different ways that you can show appreciation for others. Put a check mark by the ones that you could do.

_____ Help your parents or caregivers with chores (for example, wash the dishes, walk the dog, or set the table).

_____ Have lunch with a friend.

_____ Express your gratitude in words: "Thank you for _____!"

_____ Give someone a hug.

_____ Make a special gift (for example, a poem, a card, breakfast).

_____ Write and illustrate a gratitude story and give it to the person you're grateful for.

_____ Smile in appreciation.

_____ List what you love about yourself.

Copyright © 2022 Maureen Healy. *The Happiness Workbook for Kids*. All rights reserved.

... And More to Do

Expressing our gratitude for other people—like our teachers, parents or caregivers, friends, and neighbors—helps us become happier. Identify one person you feel grateful for, and write this person a letter thanking them.

Dear _____,

I am so happy and grateful for you. I appreciate when you:

_____

_____

_____

_____

_____

_____

Thank you,

_____

You may want to copy this page and give your letter to the person you picked—then they will share in becoming happier too! (This is not a requirement; it's up to you.)

Copyright © 2022 Maureen Healy. *The Happiness Workbook for Kids.* All rights reserved.

Ideas to Remember

The more you reach for the feeling of gratitude and find something to be thankful for, the better you feel. You can be grateful for chocolate milk, the scent of roses, or a big hug. Or you can be grateful for something or someone else. You can usually find *something* you are thankful for.

Focusing on what you're grateful for every day helps lift your mood and move you toward feeling better than before.

Copyright © 2022 Maureen Healy. *The Happiness Workbook for Kids*. All rights reserved.

Activity 19

Optimism

HAPPINESS LESSON

Optimism is looking on the bright side of life. Imagine it is raining. An optimist might say, "Awesome. I get to wear my new rain boots and splash in the puddles!" They are focusing on what feels good (positive) and choosing not to focus on the challenging (negative) part of the experience or situation.

Some days are clunkers. They just feel no good. That's normal, and you can often begin again, as we learned before. But the person who can see the positives in a negative situation is an optimist. Of course, some people are more optimistic than others, but everyone can get better at choosing to see the good things even when they're facing challenges.

Optimism is choosing to focus on the positive parts of any situation. Optimism isn't wimpy either. It takes a whole lot of courage to be optimistic in a world that often shares bad news, what you're doing wrong, and what you need to improve.

Optimistic people (both adults and children) are happier people. They see the good things, especially when others see challenges. Of course, they have challenging days too. But in general, optimistic people choose to ask: What good can come from this? Can I learn something here? What is my next best step?

Copyright © 2022 Maureen Healy. *The Happiness Workbook for Kids.* All rights reserved.

To Do

Bo's birthday party was scheduled for Saturday. His parents had arranged for a local farm to bring over animals from the petting zoo, like goats, pigs, donkeys, rabbits, and chickens. He was thrilled to have the animals, plus other treats like cotton candy and a popcorn machine. But unfortunately, Bo's party had to be rescheduled due to a thunderstorm. It was so unexpected, but there was no choice. Bo was really bummed.

Circle the optimistic thoughts Bo could think in this situation.

What a rotten, no-good thing!	We can do it another time.
Everyone is safe.	I hate this!
I still get gifts.	Things never work out for me!
More time for video games!	The animals don't have to be in the rain all day.

When things don't go our way, sometimes we feel frustrated and get angry. It's helpful to remember that when things don't go as planned, the world isn't saying "no." It's just saying "not *now*." Circle the feelings you think Bo had during this experience.

Anger	Relief
Sadness	Playfulness
Frustration	Hope
Calm	Disappointment

If you circled any of the answers, you are correct. Bo could have felt all these different emotions when he unexpectedly had to change his birthday party. At first it was a big bummer! But then Bo decided to look for the positive things that could come out of this—like maybe, he would get even more presents!

Copyright © 2022 Maureen Healy. *The Happiness Workbook for Kids*. All rights reserved.

... And More to Do

Habits are the daily things we do. For example, you likely brush your teeth every day, and that helps you feel good and take care of your body. The same is true for your mind. You need to get into the habit of feeding it positive things every day to help it see the good things.

One way to become more optimistic is to look for positive things happening right now—things you can appreciate and focus on. For example, you might say, "I ate pizza today" or "I have no homework today!"

Make a list of three good things that happened today. There are no wrong answers.

1. _____

_____

_____

2. _____

_____

_____

3. _____

_____

_____

Identifying three good things from each day will help you become more optimistic, and it ultimately moves you in a happier direction. If it's been a challenging day and it's hard to find good things, the secret is to go back to the basics and be thankful for everything. For example: "I woke up today (first good thing), my dog loves me (second good thing), and the weekend is almost here (third good thing)."

Copyright © 2022 Maureen Healy. *The Happiness Workbook for Kids*. All rights reserved.

Ideas to Remember

Choosing to be optimistic is up to you. The benefit of optimism is that it feels better and is more helpful in solving problems. Of course, optimism doesn't eliminate problems, but it helps you stay positive while you address them. Science shows that optimistic people tend to be healthier and report feeling happier too.

Optimistic captains tend to have an easier time sailing through problems (versus others who get stuck in the rainstorm). They remember to look for the good things, and they keep moving toward better-feeling thoughts and actions, while moving through the storms and challenging feelings in life.

Copyright © 2022 Maureen Healy. *The Happiness Workbook for Kids.* All rights reserved.

Helping Others

HAPPINESS LESSON

Helping others helps you become happier. Whether you help your family cook dinner, walk the dog, or tutor your friend, using your talents and energy to help others moves you in a positive-feeling direction too.

Opportunities to help others do and feel better are everywhere. You probably have heard of the "buddy bench" at some schools. It is bench placed in the recess area, and if a student feels lonely, they can sit there. By sitting there, the student is saying, "Hi, I would like a friend," and naturally other students go over to help that student feel better and be their buddy.

Buddy benches have encouraged students to be kind to one another. Every little act of kindness is important; there is no act of helping that is too small. Even rescuing a bug (who has feelings) and putting it in a place that's better for it to live is bringing that bug benefit. (Of course, you need to be careful to not get bitten or stung by harmful bugs either.)

The point is that as you help others become happier, you feel useful and usually become happier too. This is not helping that's forced. It's helping from the bottom of your heart—you truly want someone to struggle less and feel joy more.

Copyright © 2022 Maureen Healy. *The Happiness Workbook for Kids*. All rights reserved.

To Do

Helping others can take many forms. There is no limit to whom you can help, whether it's a person, an animal, a plant, or even the whole planet! We must do what we can to help every living creature live a happier life.

For now, let's focus on how you can help others this week. Place a check mark by the activities you can do.

_____ Use encouraging words, like "You've got this," "Way to go," and "You can do this!"

_____ Teach someone something.

_____ Do chores at home (take out the garbage, fold laundry, clean your room, etc.).

_____ Hold doors open for people.

_____ Compliment others.

_____ Offer to help someone (maybe someone who is elderly or not tech savvy).

_____ Listen to someone fully.

_____ Tell a joke to help someone laugh.

_____ Raise money for a cause (like people or animals in need).

_____ Find ways you can help the planet (recycling, reusing, reducing waste, etc.).

_____ Sit next to someone who is alone.

_____ Spend time playing with your dog or cat.

_____ Send a card to cheer someone up!

Helping someone else makes your heart happy. You become less focused on yourself (me, me, me) and realize that we are all in this together (we, we, we). Helping others also helps you feel better when you're in the choppy seas of life (like sadness, loss, or disappointment) because you feel useful and helpful. You want someone to feel better and, strangely, you start feeling better too.

Copyright © 2022 Maureen Healy. *The Happiness Workbook for Kids.* All rights reserved.

... And More to Do

Imagine you have a magic wand and can help someone (or a group of people, animals, or the whole planet) become better than before. You can only use your powers for good to create positive results. Whom or what would you choose to help, and why?

_____

_____

_____

_____

_____

_____

Share more of your helping "magic wand" story by drawing it here.

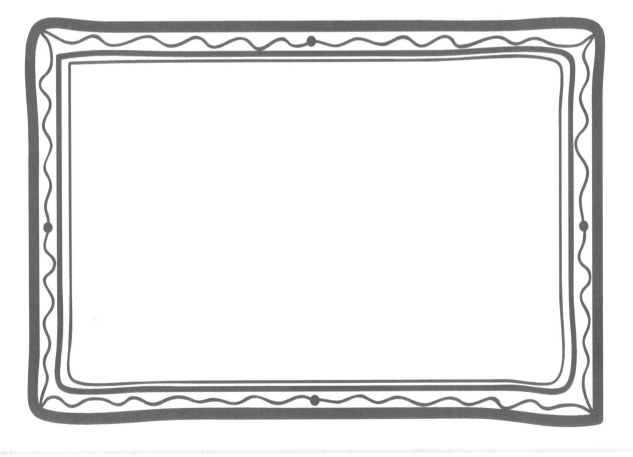

Copyright © 2022 Maureen Healy. _The Happiness Workbook for Kids._ All rights reserved.

Ideas to Remember

Helping others is an important part of becoming happier. *The more you help others, the happier you will become.* Helping takes many forms, such as:

- Kind words

- Useful actions

- Positive thoughts (or prayers)

Of course, it's also important to help yourself. The more you take care of your body and mind, the more you want others to feel good too.

Copyright © 2022 Maureen Healy. *The Happiness Workbook for Kids.* All rights reserved.

Activity 21

Reframe Challenges

HAPPINESS LESSON

We all face challenges. Although challenges are hard, they help us appreciate when things feel easier and smoother. Every challenge can teach us something (like how to be patient or brave), and we can use it as a step toward happier life experiences.

Challenges can be big or small. A big challenge might be when your best friend moves away unexpectedly. A smaller challenge might be when you stub your toe on the bed—ouch! As we grow, what seems like a big challenge at one point soon becomes something we can handle, which makes it smaller. This is how life goes.

Challenges, like emotions, sometimes have speed. They can happen quickly, like when your teacher announces that you're having a surprise test. Others take time, like when you're hiking up a mountain, and it's only after you've done five miles that the hike starts to seem like a big challenge. Whether a challenge is big or small, fast or slow, it's an opportunity to learn and to keep moving toward a happier life experiences.

Learning how to face a challenge and see the upside of it (if there is one) is helpful. Take, for example, the hike where after five miles, you're exhausted. Instead of complaining about hiking up the mountain with your family, you could instead think: "Wow, I am outside in nature hearing the birds. My body is tired, but this is good exercise. I will sleep well tonight!"

Changing how you see the situation (which is called "reframing") can help you feel better than before and make you feel strong as you set out on your path.

Copyright © 2022 Maureen Healy. *The Happiness Workbook for Kids.* All rights reserved.

To Do

Ben is ten years old and going into fifth grade. Over the summer, he's both excited and scared about going to his first sleepaway camp with friends. Some of the amazing things he'll get to do are archery, paddle boarding, kayaking, riding horses, feeding the chickens, and whittling (carving things from wood). He's never done any of these. What he's nervous about is sleeping away from home for the first time.

Below are some of the thoughts Ben is having. Read each thought, and decide whether or not he has reframed the challenge by looking at the positives.

1. I'm so excited for all my new adventures!   Reframe   Nope

2. I just cannot do this.   Reframe   Nope

3. I won't be able to sleep.   Reframe   Nope

4. This is a great opportunity for me to be more independent. Reframe   Nope

5. I will probably be so tired at night and sleep like a baby. Reframe   Nope

6. No one can help me.   Reframe   Nope

7. I will be surrounded by friends and camp counselors who   Reframe   Nope
    care about me. This is going to be great!

Ben is learning how to think more positively and reframe his challenges. At camp, Ben can feel more independent, enjoy all the fun activities, and lean on his friends and the camp counselors if he needs assistance. Of course, with some challenges, it's not so easy to find the good parts—but if we look, oftentimes we can find something positive, even if it's learning how to be patient or kind.

Copyright © 2022 Maureen Healy. *The Happiness Workbook for Kids.* All rights reserved.

... And More to Do

Challenges come in all shapes and sizes. Some common challenges are listed here. Circle the ones that you've experienced (whether recently or a long time ago).

Being teased	Having a tummy ache
Forgetting your homework	Fighting with a friend
Getting punished	Hurting yourself
Going to the hospital	Spilling something on yourself
Stepping in dog doo-doo	Feeling left out
Failing a test	Not making a team or activity
Losing a game	Feeling worried
Feeling embarrassed	Breaking something by accident
Having bad dreams	Falling in front of others

Chances are good that you circled some of these challenges. The next step is to take one of these challenges (or another one that you think of) and find the positive parts of the experience. For example, if you keep forgetting your homework, maybe it's an opportunity to get more organized—so you decide to buy a special folder, make a checklist, and set an alarm every day to remind you! Pick a small challenge to start. Ask for help, if needed.

What is your challenge?

_____

_____

What is the upside? (What good can come from this? What can you learn?)

_____

_____

Copyright © 2022 Maureen Healy. *The Happiness Workbook for Kids*. All rights reserved.

Ideas to Remember

Challenges happen to everyone. You can feel angry, sad, and disappointed in yourself (or others) when a challenge pops up. But never lose hope. There will be better days. Others can help you overcome challenges, and you can build your skills of being strong from the inside out.

One important way to overcome challenges is to see the positive side of the challenge. For example, if you have ever been bullied, you have a deeper understanding of what bullying feels like, and you likely would never bully anyone else because you know how terrible it feels. You want others to feel better. Reframing your challenges like this helps you feel better and make smarter choices.

Copyright © 2022 Maureen Healy. *The Happiness Workbook for Kids*. All rights reserved.

Use Your Talents

HAPPINESS LESSON

Using your unique talents makes you happier. When you use your talents, you also often lose track of time and feel "in the flow." Of course, it's important to be on time for school and other things. But the more you do what you love and use your unique talents, the happier you become.

Every person has a unique talent that they bring to the world—something they discover they're naturally good at. This doesn't mean they're perfect at it, though. We all need to practice and learn from others to develop our talents. For example, even basketball legend Michael Jordan had to practice a great deal before he became a sports superstar.

Your unique talents could be in a school subject, a sport, or another activity, or even something that you won't find on a report card or trophy, like helping others. Of course, your interests can change as you grow. But if you have one interest, like science, it may eventually lead you to something even greater, like helping to solve the climate crisis and assist our planet. One step at a time.

Using our unique talents for good makes us happier. That's because spending time doing what you love makes you feel happier. And by sharing your unique talents, you can help others too. Let's take some time now to think about the special gifts you can give to the world. There is no end to the possibilities!

Copyright © 2022 Maureen Healy. *The Happiness Workbook for Kids.* All rights reserved.

To Do

Exploring what interests you can be a lot of fun. Of course, sometimes we discover what we're *not* interested in too. This is normal. The point is to enjoy the journey of discovering what you uniquely bring to the world, and then muster the courage to share your unique gifts for the greater good.

Put a check mark by the items that you're interested in:

_____ Archery	_____ Nature
_____ Speaking different languages	_____ Dinosaurs
_____ Helping other people or animals	_____ Sewing
_____ Cooking	_____ Painting
_____ Gymnastics	_____ Building computers
_____ Video games	_____ Inventing things
_____ Music	_____ Ancient civilizations
_____ Unicorns, rainbows, magic	_____ Oceans, rivers, lakes
_____ Skateboarding or cycling	_____ Sports
_____ Museums	_____ Acting
_____ Putting things together	_____ Swimming
_____ Reading and writing	_____ Stars, galaxies
_____ Woodworking	_____ Camping
_____ Horseback riding	_____ Watching movies
_____ Fashion and clothes	_____ Growing vegetables
_____ Building robots	_____ Having a lemonade stand

What are some other things you're interested in?

_____

_____

_____

_____

Copyright © 2022 Maureen Healy. *The Happiness Workbook for Kids.* All rights reserved.

... And More to Do

Imagine you can create anything. You might want to solve a problem, bring others happiness, or have fun. What would you create or invent? Draw it here.

What did you create or invent?

_____

_____

What would you need to make this in real life? Which of your talents would you use? Would you need to develop additional skills?

_____

_____

_____

_____

Copyright © 2022 Maureen Healy. *The Happiness Workbook for Kids.* All rights reserved.

Ideas to Remember

Discovering your unique talents happens over time. You may discover that you're athletic when you're younger, but then when you're older, you might realize that you're good at speaking multiple languages or performing surgery. Give yourself time to find your unique talents—there's no rush, really! Allow yourself the time to explore many different things and to pursue what you absolutely love, whether it's wildlife photography or making the best waffles.

The good news is that there is room for everyone's talents, and every person on the planet can contribute to the greater good. Plus, this helps you become happier too.

Copyright © 2022 Maureen Healy. *The Happiness Workbook for Kids.* All rights reserved.

Friends

HAPPINESS LESSON

Having friends helps us become happier. They make us laugh, listen to us, and enjoy our company. Life without friends can feel lonely. Choosing our friends wisely is important because they become our extended family. People with friends are healthier and live longer too.

Friends are the sprinkles of life. They make everything more enjoyable and fun. You may have friends at school, in your neighborhood, and on your sports team or in your other activities. You can also make new friends throughout your life.

A real friend is nice to you, respects you, tells you the truth, is trustworthy, and might have similar interests as you. If someone isn't nice to you regularly, this person isn't your friend. Of course, a friend can have a bad day, but that doesn't happen often, and they apologize afterward.

Becoming a good friend is beneficial to everyone. You help others become happier, and you become happier too. There is no one on the planet who doesn't need a friend (even animals need friends too!). Choosing your friends carefully is important, so let's talk more about what makes a good friend.

Copyright © 2022 Maureen Healy. *The Happiness Workbook for Kids*. All rights reserved.

To Do

Some of us have wonderful friends, while others of us would like new friends. Imagine you are placing an order with the universe for a wonderful friend. What would that friend be like? Circle all that apply.

Honest	Funny
Trustworthy	Kind
Nice	Smart
Happy	Forgiving
Creative	Generous
Adventurous	Playful
Helpful	Nonjudgmental

What else might you want in a friend?

_____

_____

_____

_____

Copyright © 2022 Maureen Healy. *The Happiness Workbook for Kids.* All rights reserved.

... And More to Do

How do friends make you happier? Think of a friend you have now (or someone you had as a friend). Tell me how this relationship helped you. (Furry friends count, too!)

Name the friend:

_____

How long have you known this friend?

_____

What have you done together?

_____

_____

_____

How has this friend cheered you up?

_____

_____

_____

How does this friend make you laugh?

_____

_____

_____

How else does this friend make you happier?

_____

_____

_____

Copyright © 2022 Maureen Healy. *The Happiness Workbook for Kids.* All rights reserved.

... And a Bonus To-Do!

Friendships include give-and-take. That means sometimes you help your friend, and sometimes they help you. Other times you help each other at the same time, whether it's having fun, enjoying life, or completing homework. The point is that making and keeping good friends requires time and effort.

Read this short story, and answer the questions afterward:

> Luca is in fifth grade and just turned ten years old. He had a big birthday party with a mariachi band, make-your-own tacos, and a piñata. His best friends—Kyle, Billy, and Bao—were having fun. At one point, Luca told Bao that he failed the last two math quizzes and really needs some help from someone. Bao offered to help him study for the next quiz, which ended up being the best birthday gift ever.

Is Bao a good friend to help Luca?

      Yes   No   Unsure

Do friends, in general, help each other?

      Yes   No   Unsure

Was Luca talking about his math struggles with Bao because he trusted him as a friend?

      Yes   No   Unsure

Are real friendships based on trust and honesty?

      Yes   No   Unsure

Do you have a real friendship in your life?

      Yes   No   Unsure

Copyright © 2022 Maureen Healy. *The Happiness Workbook for Kids*. All rights reserved.

Ideas to Remember

We all need friends (adults too). The basis of friendship is trust and honesty. A good friend is trustworthy and is nice to you. Of course, anyone can have a bad day, but a good friend will apologize when they make a mistake. The same goes for you.

Having good friends helps you become happier. You get to share your good times, as well as your challenges. Sometimes you help your friends and sometimes they help you. The best type of friends can help you laugh too!

Copyright © 2022 Maureen Healy. *The Happiness Workbook for Kids.* All rights reserved.

The Ripple Effect

HAPPINESS LESSON

Imagine you toss a rock into a river. The rock lands, and the water around it creates ripples (waves) as it sinks. That one act of throwing the rock has an impact on the water around it. Just like the rock created this ripple effect in the water, *your choices impact others*. When you make smart choices, they have a more positive impact—on both yourself and others.

One day, Charlie woke up to see that her dad had made her favorite pancakes! She was so grateful. She immediately thanked him—and ate every single one. On the way to the bus stop, she couldn't help but smile. Charlie said, "Good morning!" to her bus driver, Ed, and smiled at all the kids on the bus. It was as if everyone around her became happier because she spread her kindness out in words, thoughts, and actions.

Using her energy to spread kindness created a positive ripple effect. Ed, the bus driver, felt so good after his morning drive that he went directly to the store and bought his wife, Kelly, a whole bunch of flowers. Then Kelly was feeling so good that she decided to make Ed's favorite dinner that night. The ripple effect is real.

Of course, we can also have a not-so-good ripple effect. Imagine that Charlie had a whole different day. She woke up and stubbed her toe. Then she yelled at her dad, and he decided to make her toast, which he accidentally burnt. The ripple effect would continue unless Charlie decided to turn her "emotional boat" around, which she could totally choose to do at any point.

The important point is that we are largely in control of our actions—and what ripple effect we create. Certainly, some days feel better than others, and some things are outside of our control, but we get to choose how we respond to life events. We can't always be happy, but we can always do our best—and hopefully create many positive ripple effects.

Copyright © 2022 Maureen Healy. *The Happiness Workbook for Kids*. All rights reserved.

To Do

Think of a positive thing (words or action) you can do, and imagine how it might help others feel good too (a ripple effect). Examples include: having the class over to your house for a pool or camping party, holding the door open for someone, or saying good morning to the grumpy principal.

What positive thing can you say or do, and how could this create positive-feeling waves (ripples) for another person or a group of people?

_____

_____

_____

Draw this same idea as a comic strip, telling the story of your positive waves.

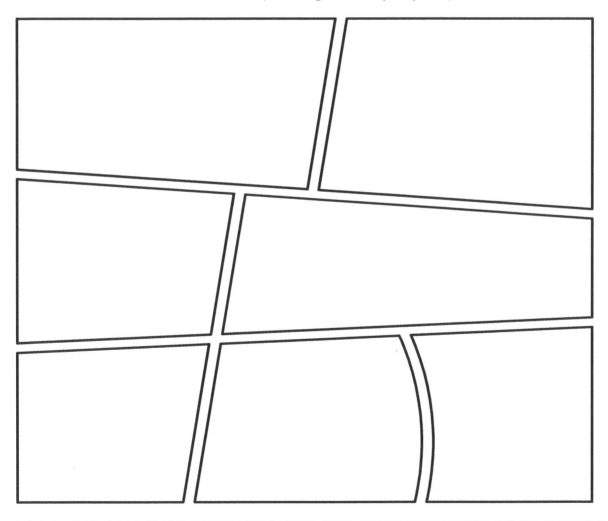

... And More to Do

Can you think of a time when someone was super nice to you? Maybe someone brought cookies to class and shared them with you. Or your parents took you on a trip to a theme park. Or someone gave you a great big compliment and said how wonderful you are at playing the piano (or something else).

Describe what this person did or said that made you feel good.

_____

_____

_____

_____

_____

You may want to draw it here too.

You experienced the ripple effect of someone else's positive choices!

Copyright © 2022 Maureen Healy. *The Happiness Workbook for Kids*. All rights reserved.

Ideas to Remember

Our words and actions impact others. There is no one on the planet who doesn't experience the effects of others (including animals, oceans, trees, and more!). Without a doubt, *you can have a positive impact on yourself and others*, which can move you in a happier direction.

Remember, you're the captain of your emotional ship, and you can sail anywhere you choose. Enjoy it all.

Copyright © 2022 Maureen Healy. *The Happiness Workbook for Kids*. All rights reserved.

Key Lessons

· · · · · · · · · · · ·

- You're learning how to become the boss of your emotions.

- There are no bad emotions.

- Emotions are signals that point to what's happening inside you.

- Emotions are felt in your body but seen by the outside world.

- There are positive (helpful) emotions and negative (challenging) emotions.

- All emotions are temporary. They come to visit, but not to stay.

- Thoughts and emotions are connected. You can think a new thought to get a new feeling.

- Smart choices are good for you and good for others.

- Paying attention to your feelings before they get enormous is helpful.

- There are many strategies that can help you come back to center when you feel emotionally off-balance. Some examples are doing breathing exercises, drawing, jumping on a trampoline, or talking to someone.

- Becoming happier is a skill you can learn.

- There are certain things you can think, say, or do to become happier.

- One key to becoming happier is learning how to be kind, which includes being kind to yourself too.

- You have the power within you to create your happiest life ever.

Copyright © 2022 Maureen Healy. *The Happiness Workbook for Kids.* All rights reserved.

The Happiness Pledge

• • • • • • • • • • • •

I am a powerful creator.

I can create happier life experiences for myself and others.

Today is the first day of my happier life.

My happier life includes:

- Being kind

- Being honest

- Being strong

- Making smart choices

- Helping others

- Having fun

I choose happier today so that good comes my way.

Today is a happy day!

Copyright © 2022 Maureen Healy. *The Happiness Workbook for Kids*. All rights reserved.

Answer Key

· · · · · · · · · · · ·

Activity 1

Sad:	Unhappy, blue
Angry:	Mad, furious
Happy:	Joyful, glad
Frustrated:	Irritated, annoyed
Brave:	Courageous, strong
Excited:	Enthusiastic, eager
Scared:	Afraid, fearful
Shy:	Timid, bashful
Sleepy:	Tired, fatigued
Embarrassed:	Awkward, humiliated
Confident:	Sure of oneself, cool
Curious:	Interested, eager to learn
Generous:	Giving, sharing

Activity 3

Sophia:	Everyone is bad in the beginning.
	If I practice more, I'll get better.
Noah:	I'm brave today.
	I only need one friend to start.
Jemima:	They all sound funny to me too.
	I'm going to make a friend who loves my accent.

Activity 12

Sadness:	The feeling of being unhappy
Worry:	The feeling of concern and nervousness
Anger:	The feeling of intense frustration (feeling mad)
Frustration:	The feeling of not liking how things are
Jealousy:	The feeling of wanting what someone else has
Disgust:	The feeling of disapproval and yuckiness
Overwhelm:	The feeling of too many things at once

Activity 14

Relief:	The feeling of stress going away
Gratitude:	The feeling of thankfulness
Confidence:	The feeling that you can do it
Enthusiasm:	The feeling of excitement
Calmness:	The feeling of peace and quiet
Self-love:	The feeling of loving yourself
Silliness:	The feeling of being goofy and funny
Joy:	The feeling of happiness

Activity 17

Rory:	It will be fun to buy or borrow different clothes and change it up.
	I'm so happy to be alive and okay!
Josie:	Mom's doctors are the best in the world.
	After the surgery, Mom will feel better (and so will I).
Maya:	We all drop things. It's normal.
	It was a little funny, I bet.

Activity 19

Bo: Everyone is safe.

I still get gifts.

More time for video games!

We can do it another time.

The animals don't have to be in the rain all day.

Activity 21

1. Reframe
2. Nope
3. Nope
4. Reframe
5. Reframe
6. Nope
7. Reframe

Gratitude

· · · · · · · · · · · · ·

I am so blessed and grateful to be here today. I'm especially thankful to my parents, who valued education and learning as an essential part of becoming healthier and happier. Additionally, I am so thankful for my teachers—in little bodies and bigger ones—for keeping me healthy and helping me remember the way toward a happier life.

One thing I know for sure is that becoming happier is possible for nearly anyone. My hope is that the children who use this book gain some direct experiences and "emotional aha" moments so they can move in a happier direction. In other words, I hope to plant the seeds of happier life experiences and help them avoid the unnecessary bumps of life.

Also, I would be remiss without thanking the children around the world who have given me the privilege of helping them, which added to my happiness bucket. My hope is that I have added to their happiness buckets too.

About the Author

Maureen Healy is an award-winning author, popular speaker, and expert in children's emotional health and education. Her last book, *The Emotionally Healthy Child*, had a preface from the Dalai Lama, who said, "I hope Maureen's book will contribute to a more wholesome education for future generations." Healy is also the author of *Growing Happy Kids: How to Foster Inner Confidence, Success, and Happiness* and *The Energetic Keys to Indigo Kids*. In addition, she contributes to a popular blog on *Psychology Today* and has appeared across all media outlets.

Unique about Maureen is her global experience—working with children from the Bronx in New York City all the way to the base of the Himalayas. Her background in child development (BA, MBA, PhD program), complemented by her global studies with happiness teachers, has empowered her path to help children worldwide learn the ideas and strategies of becoming happier in their lifetime. To learn more about Maureen or to get in contact with her, visit growinghappykids.com.

Further Reading

· · · · · · · · · · · ·

For your convenience, purchasers can download and print
the worksheets from www.pesi.com/Healy

Books for Kids

Breathe Like a Bear: 30 Mindful Moments for Kids to Feel Calm and Focused Anytime, Anywhere by Kira Willey; illustrated by Anni Betts

This book provides 30 activities to help young children direct their breath and feel calmer.

Growing Friendships: A Kids' Guide to Making and Keeping Friends by Eileen Kennedy-Moore and Christine McLaughlin

This book is for children who need a little extra guidance on what friends really are and how to make—as well as keep—real friends.

Have You Filled a Bucket Today?: A Guide to Daily Happiness for Kids by Carol McCloud; illustrated by David Messing

This book helps children learn how to be kind to themselves and others as a key route toward happier experiences.

Just Breathe: Meditation, Mindfulness, Movement, and More by Mallika Chopra; illustrated by Brenna Vaughn

This book focuses on helping middle school–aged students to learn how to calm, center, and make better choices when life is challenging.

Mindfulness for Kids in 10 Minutes a Day: Simple Exercises to Feel Calm, Focused, and Happy by Maura Bradley

This book helps children learn how to use mindfulness to calm and make good choices despite the challenges of life.

Mindfulness Workbook for Kids: 60+ Activities to Focus, Stay Calm, and Make Good Choices by Hannah Sherman

This workbook for children increases their ability to self-regulate and make responsible choices.

The Seed of Compassion: Lessons from the Life and Teachings of His Holiness the Dalai Lama by His Holiness the Dalai Lama; illustrated by Bao Luu

This book is for younger readers to learn what compassion is and how it is central to happier life experiences.

Books for Adults

The Book of Joy: Lasting Happiness in a Changing World by His Holiness the Dalai Lama and Archbishop Desmond Tutu with Douglas Abrams

This comprehensive book shares the roots of joy from wisdom to western science.

The Childhood Roots of Adult Happiness: Five Steps to Help Kids Create and Sustain Lifelong Joy by Edward M. Hallowell

This book shares how to positively impact a child's ability to feel joy.

The Emotionally Healthy Child: Helping Children Calm, Center, and Make Smarter Choices by Maureen Healy

This book is focused on the essential ideas and strategies children need to regulate their emotions and to move toward—not away from—happier life experiences.

Growing Happy Kids: How to Foster Inner Confidence, Success, and Happiness by Maureen Healy

This book offers a five-step program to help adults nurture inner confidence and resilience in their children.

Happier: Learn the Secrets to Daily Joy and Lasting Fulfillment by Tal Ben-Shahar

This book explores the research on happiness and how adults and children can live happier lives.

Happy Teachers Change the World: A Guide for Cultivating Mindfulness in Education by Thich Nhat Hanh and Katherine Weare

This book shows how mindfulness is connected to happiness. It teaches educators how to use mindfulness practices to facilitate their own happiness as well as their students'.